JACKIE WILLS has published six collections of poetry, a collection of essays and a guide to running workshops, *On Poetry* (Smith Doorstop, 2023), and short stories. Shortlisted for the 1995 T. S. Eliot Prize, she was included in *Mslexia*'s top ten women poets of the decade in 2004 and received a Cholmondeley Award in 2023. Judge Moniza Alvi wrote: 'Jackie Wills is a very natural, genuine poet of sensitivity, boldness and flair. She has been writing explorative, compassionate and often mesmerising poetry for many years. Wills explores with grace and verve what it is to be human.'

AF194380

JACKIE WILLS
Making the Wedding Dress

SALT

CROMER

PUBLISHED BY SALT PUBLISHING 2026

2 4 6 8 10 9 7 5 3 1

First published in Great Britain in 2026 by
Salt Publishing Ltd
12 Norwich Road, Cromer, NR27 0AX United Kingdom
www.saltpublishing.com

GPSR representative
Matt Parsons matt.parsons@upi2mbooks.hr
UPI-2M PLUS d.o.o., Medulićeva 20, 10000 Zagreb, Croatia

Salt Publishing Limited Reg. No. 5293401

A CIP catalogue record for this book is available from the British Library

ISBN 978 1 78463 384 4 (Paperback edition)

Typeset in Sabon by Salt Publishing

Printed and bound in Great Britain by Clays Ltd, Elcograf S.p.A.

Contents

Silk

Modern living has still found no escape from the loose button, the pulled-out hem, the broken strap or the cigarette burn in a new garment.

McCall's Sewing in Colour

How to mend a sheet

shake out the old, white
cotton, hold it to the light

in places it's thin as a veil
soft as muslin, it strains

the sun to jelly through tracery
worn by bodies –

measure that body-wear,
its depth, the square

where love's rolled away
blotting out day –

measure a patch from a scrap, fit
it over the space love's worn thin –

find thread strong enough
for all the nights to come –

a fine needle, slippery
as the waters of sleep

to mimic the sea rebuilding reefs
mending itself and your belief

Shrine to broken needles

like a seamstress visiting
a shrine to broken needles

pressing each ruined point
into a cake of tofu

thanking scissors, thimbles, thread
for their service while a priest

honours needles with sutras,
she returns each year

to Sainsbury's car park
to hear a nightingale sing

Ripped pleat

to reinforce, embroider an arrowhead or a crow's foot tack

crow a watchman of graves behind our house   caw beneath
the dove's coo   it was there at the graveyard gates when boys
kicking a ball brought men in stab jackets   eight of them to
question six nine-year-olds   to chase a five-year-old up the
pavement home   copying names in notebooks   my hand
a crow's foot tack   I'd have stitched a murder of them to
keep my son   from those men

Skin

loosened by tranquilliser I stare into
the surgeon's bone-china face
as she snips at mine

scrapes away a carcinoma
cuts a patch
behind my ear

her stitches will be neat as a tailor
no shakes yet
no carelessness

she lays a dressing over her needlework
the size, shape, of an egg
keep it dry, she says

an egg no one will see
in flat, stitched lowlands by my nose
until it heals

and I'll wait with others like me
(all our eggs bloodied, stained)
for the reveal

Little stabs (sashiko)

on the morning of the first frost
after breaking ice in the birds' water

I make little stabs in a patch –
sewing lines of white dashes like steps

in the ladder I leaned into a tree
to pick plums – the tree catching

my sleeve as if to tell me something
before plums dropped into my bag

Broken shoulder strap

think of a bra, the weight a strap holds
bags of flesh braced in two cones
and you might wonder what a woman draws
out of herself lying on her side
her baby's head crooked in an arm
small hours leaking at a cry
think of the shoulder's work to remain
upright, carry a strap to each breast
the endless litres a woman makes
the names a bra is christened with

A neighbour and a darn

It's my first chance to commiserate
we stand apart in the street
her dog pulls at its lead
she looks at a crucifix
on a roof, offers it her sorrows.

She's planning to move.
I see chalk paths cross her eyes
certain as stitches.
Refocussing, she looks at my elbow,
I like your darns.

I lift my arms, turn around,
a neighbour found it on a wall
it's Sisley, mohair, warm.
I'm not sure why I twirl and boast –
we talk of repairs, woodworm,
gulls nesting between chimney pots.

I feel useless, she says.
Our time of life lifts us
above the pavement
until everything passes
underneath. Perhaps we shiver
like saints, perhaps
we're blurred to people
below – who knows –
but I'm in my mended jumper,
she can see the Downs,
we wish ourselves luck.

The needle's protection

A woman bends over cloth
in light cold as a freezer –
embroiders deer over burns on a sleeve,
water lilies float in a stain
her silk paradise is made for the tomb.

She lays an unconscious mother
in a border of fierce wild roses
to carry on sleeping.
Her seams must be strong.
Her fingers sure of their work.

Edges

The tailor bird chooses a leaf
and wraps herself in it

as you'd try on a shawl,
looking sideways

at your reflection,
holding edges together.

She rivets two hundred stitches
with cotton, wool and insect silk,

as a mother might, one evening,
prepare herself.

Dressmaker at the market

I stop at the dressmaker's stall
to ask what she does with leftovers.
We discuss bunting – it's a slow day.
I buy a £10 bag of scraps, swatches,
snippets, interrupted patterns
and borders. The bag taps a Morse
of promises against my leg – eyes
outlined in gold thread, dots, dashes,
all the birds of the world in repeated
murmurations and mating dances,
lines of ladders to the moon: promises
as they're meant to be. They unravel noisily –
metres of cloth anticipating weddings,
funerals, birthdays. My bag of patches
and irregular lines makes do, invents a flag
of no particular country, resurrects a hand
from the place an arm was cut to conduct
more songs of love, redemption, surrender.

Leaving with the wedding dress

for Giya

At the station an LED sign tells passengers
thousands of geese will pass over the country
today in their migration, and leaving Rotterdam,

in the sky above my train, I watch four chevrons
of them above a wet field of sheep that don't look up,
swans neither, or the herons, moorhens, ducks –

not a single keeper of the place looks up
at the start of my passage home, leaving
my daughter, carrying the first version

of her wedding dress I've made in cheap cotton,
grey as these chevrons, standing water, clouds –
the dress knowing its journey, as I do.

Note

The work *Arrivals / Departures* by Marcus Coates hangs at Utrecht
Centraal station in the Netherlands.

Making the wedding dress

a child took its mother, leading her by the hand

It's the oldest work and this dress,
in ivory dupion and organza,
is pegged with notes on where
to take care. I'm new to silk

but you brought me to its feather touch,
its drift to earth. I hold a section of skirt
to the window, arrange the five-part
bodice, sleeves like empty maps.

I see you crossing countries.
I'm learning silk's tendency to fray,
but mostly how it catches light,
like you. As I stitch I think of places silk

has travelled through. When I began,
unrolled metres for cutting, I found a footprint
on the back. The world knew where
to leave a message for you.

Epigraph from *Wild Conquest* by Peter Abrahams

Dyeing the wedding dress

So many metres of silk must be worn for more than a day.
After puzzling over the pattern's engineering, after cutting
the bodice wrong, days of hand-stitching, tacking, ironing,
all the zigzagging and covering seams to prevent fraying,
after the two toiles you tried, after you put it on for real
at home with friends, after photos, promises, speeches,
flowers, toasts, bunting, the band, your sister singing,
your brother on piano, playing you in to all our tears –

no cupboard can hold all that. I say, *I'll take the risk,*
I'll dye it. I've asked every question, about shrinkage,
colour, temperature. We shop together as we did before.
You're away when I pull it out of the machine – the colour
of tulips I bought at the market – two bunches for your flat,
the purest yellow opening in the sun like full skirts.

Sinkhole

when someone mentions the ancient philosophers

I see them beachcombing – Heraclitus, Socrates, Plato,
Aristotle – kicking mounds of seaweed, uncovering

dogfish corpses, stems from underwater forests. I hear
the desperate percussion of boots on shingle, debates

on justice, reality, what is weakness? Is it a need
in late afternoon for something sweet? I hear them

discuss the unfamiliar path, when that heron over there
is so certain of its flight between the estuary

and somewhere else . . . stones are so hard to walk on
boxers build the shoreline into their training.

The philosophers are long gone, their works unknown
to most of us, unexamined as seaweed after a storm,

but perhaps somewhere they clap hearing their names,
chanting no, but, no, but, look, look, look, look!

Escape

When the farmer left with a vanful of young rams
all the mothers ran into the woods. And like them,
I wandered the island, missing the missing,
replaying the van's tyres on the track like fireworks.
Without them the valley sulked, I slipped,
twisting my knee. The wind was cold on the terraces.
I found an abandoned herb garden, picked lavender
tall as a stone wall, crimson salvia, a new sage.
I carried my fist of red like a flag, crushed leaves
to a volatile oil not quite of urine between thumb and finger –

a trace I couldn't identify, emptiness, perhaps, a maze?
I heard, before I saw them on the same track the van took,
pine woods to their right, Tower of Souls behind,
a choir of ewes, ears ripped by the wild dog,
fleeces snagged by brambles. They came to the house,
gathered round my car and followed me back to their fields,
nudging my tray of grain, butting and pushing
to be close, filing with me through the gate, ringing
bells that scribbled their path between rocks,
back in the garden where they'd fed their lambs.

Often alone

I grub a remedy for being one
        hunt missing limbs that slept with mine
the *we* I never use in company
        the single woman I am with two or four or six.

What cure for being one in such a coupled
        cast? Dresses only I have an opinion on,
rosemary, sage, garlic on my hands
        and me, a window, rattling.

I cheer the others on – it seems right –
        alone night enters my room,
ushering families of foxes from the street,
        herring gulls, graveyard bats,

slowworms that escaped the cat,
        grasshoppers in grass I haven't cut,
solitary queen bumble bees. Do we commune?
        No human words are fit.

The price of meteorites

In my collection of space rock – journey time impossible to
calculate – the smallest is unexceptional as walking, ordinary
as words or sprats in oceans. I understand that to calculate
the number of meteorite fragments on earth is conjecture.
I'll outbid any collector to make a 3D jigsaw of eternity –
bargaining with nomads in deserts for falls they witness out
of emptiness into emptiness.

Someone has sent me a sinkhole

that will swallow my water butts
sparrows in my fuchsia

all the broken keyboards
in my cellar –

it will take my house down.
The sinkhole curses earth, rain,

earth, rain. It moans,
laments. *I'm your future*,

my sinkhole warns.
There's a curse tablet made of lead

someone wants to bind me to,
throw into a drain, a grave.

the night before I turn seventy

Sixty-nine ticks off its minutes. The cat feels it,
pawing me as I prepare to demolish my desk,
toolbox heavy on the stairs as water lugged uphill.

That evening before my son was ten the curve
of nine was so roundly human it sat listening
to a story. *I don't want to be ten,* he said.

It was fine, June was hot, we ate ice cream.
I'm turning in mid-winter. It's a night for destruction.
I lever nails, unscrew dusty heads, ease off the frame.

My desk donates a pair of cabinets to the bed.
They stand on either side, relatives at a wake,
shelves, top, exterior panels, unsure of what to do

but mourn. The base remembers being a washstand
in another century and they're reminiscing
about bodies bowing towards a bowl of water,

rubbing soap into suds. They've half-forgotten skin
and its vanities. The scrape of a razor, a cut. Planets
hum like a chorus of women whose job is to explain.

Talk in the poolside sauna

Around me, blue tattoos all over two torsos,
several shoulders. In the family search I found
FAREWELL ERIN on Thomas Kelly from Cork,
with three hearts and crossed bones. William Platt
had GOOD LUCK nesting with a snake, dragon,
bird and butterfly. The talk today in the sauna
is wrinkles, who's had Botox, who looks younger
(everyone) than their years. I guess they haven't noticed
I'm here, blue veins bulging from my right leg,
which might do as a tattoo, a scar on my arm
four inches long, I'll claim is from a fight. Untrue.
Wrinkles are taboo, so that makes me taboo
and I think of all that truly was taboo back then.
I marched, bought books, shouted not against wrinkles
but the right, I guess, for anyone to live long enough
to wear them as they choose. A woman praises youth,
but *who takes risks like I did?* asks a man whose body
is a graphic novel. I don't butt in. I stare at a glass
corridor opposite where BLAZE is written large
in red neon. It projects lines on the pool
each swimmer crosses unwittingly, so every other
length's another finish. What can I say about wrinkles?
They mark my face, neck, hands, and yes I'm guilty
of neglect but if we're talking about the body – we know
it's mostly water – can it choose what it reflects?

Every other day

I try and swim. I breathe and push to stay alive. Upstairs –
levers, weights, a static bike with screen
is playing sun-bleached rocks. I stay alive
in fifteen-minute slots. The pool's edged with heated
rooms – sauna, steam. Every other day I try and swim.

It takes my mind off what I am, the body I inhabit, the fact
of being human at this time. There's little chat, I park the car
in daylight, leave in the dark, move my arms and legs,
imitating frogs, as I was taught. I hope my blood moves
as it should. Who knows what corvids will gather in my sleep
to peck at chains and coins, gossip with gulls about my human faults,
or if the wine will wake me up at three. The water reveals legs
and torsos mostly edged in black. This sunken place is warm at least.

I know many swim more than me. Terrapins, squid, cloaks of sardines.
There's just a wall between us. Outside a storm crashes on shingle,
unloads remains of cuttlefish in bladderwrack with tampon applicators
and line. Every other day I choose to swim in here – I don't belong
out there. I've known pools in gorges, twin lakes I grew up near,
their drownings, glacial streams, the rocky plunge below a secret
waterfall in another hemisphere. I choose this weightlessness,
the water self-contained where I can breathe, and underwater, scream.

I kick, I do not think, don't calculate how far I've been.
I watch the clock, shower, dry myself and dress. When I reach my car
I see the shoe prints on a wall as if they've run at right angles
to the floor, defying gravity, conjuring the oldest marks,
made when a song was sung deep down, in firelight, in a womb of rock.
And whatever happens now, I'm beginning to believe the flocks, herds,

shoals will throng again in schools, swarm and shake the earth,
so what's left of us feel a drumming in our feet, fall to our knees
at shrines to nettle spirits, buff-tailed bumblebees.

The older woman as distressed security

Something hangs over an older woman
the way columns of small flies hover
in a damp field. She let all those tones of black,
from green to purple, drain out of her hair –

her white head upset with ghosts,
its decades kettled in unruly crowds.
Yet there is a buyer, dressed as a bailiff,
knocking at her haunted, ruined house.

Offshore

That summer a super yacht cruised our beach as if looking for the way – its cargo, people smaller than I could see. Too big to enter the marina, stranded offshore, it turned into an island. Behind, a wind farm stepped out of line like kids on an outing. There was no wind. Every turbine was static. Disposable barbecues sent out smoke signals celebrating warm Kronenbourg 1664, Morrisons coleslaw. Portable speakers went head to head. On the island money was busy changing names, unstoppable as falling in love, which many of us were doing on shore – swimming past the limits of land. Catching our breath, bathers and lovers, we wondered at the boat, its operatic name, its coded exits and entrances, the absence of cats or loose change. Its invisible passengers watched us back through a daze of burning meat and vegan substitutes – so many real people laid out on the stones.

Seller of nutmeg graters

My pitch is a photographer's one shot of a megacity, all colours, consumables, market stalls and the central blur of mopeds. At the exact moment the shutter opens it vacuums my soul, a small egg of hard wood I use to demonstrate, the tang it releases, powder for milk and apples, its resin and healing astringency. That exact moment is the time millions write next to a name (someone born or dead), a train missed with all its consequences, a meeting in a place like this, at a crossing between stalls where people buy and sell the stillness of each second, wrap it around their heads and shoulders, eat, drink and spray it, wondering where it's gone. With me, sellers of walking sticks, laces, dog collars, matches, long songs, cures, tracts and green stuff.

Fields

for Sue Wicks

All the farmers I see on my way home
are ploughing, furrowing the dark soil
of northern Europe from the Netherlands
through Belgium to France.

Tractors turn mud over in lines. In one field
there are three, as if a klaxon's rung
and they've rolled out of barns
on big tyres, orange cab lights flashing

in the short afternoon. Mist sits
watching behind boundaries of poplars,
in copses awarded leave to remain
'til the law changes again.

Once I would have praised this time,
fields being turned over. I believed
only graveyards should be undisturbed.
Yet these straight lines,

everyone out at the same time. . .
A man clicks his keyboard,
a kid kicks my seat, the border force
asks what I've been doing –

I have to gag myself. There's no going back.
Cab lights attempt to blink an answer.
Something revolves into a flash. So many
per second. Field turns on field.

The emptiness

When I rented out my daughter's room
the first woman to stay was days from giving birth.
My children forgot their books and models,
their father his vinyl and percussion. Two cats,
two rabbits left, the dog. A fledgling wren
died in my palm. Emptiness claimed the sounds
that trailed them, growls and leaps, claws on wood,
warnings from the trees, scales blown into a reed,
hammered onto strings, rhythms played by hands
on goat skin. I was born in a month over-familiar
with emptiness when rain overwhelms gutters
in its rush for a void, singing a phrase that translated
means *emptiness holds its shape until it finds another.*
I could be there, a deserted palace garden overlooked
by storks or on a midnight road, driving into the glare
of a full moon, owls flying low towards the car.

My Welsh grandmother conjures her future
from *The Imperial-Royal Dream Book*

I never knew Gladys Powell, just her broken book of fate,
its pencil marks, missing spine, loose and torn page 129.
It stole Gertrude's mourning wail among the flowers,
One woe shall tread upon another's heels, so fast they follow . . .
lifted Shakespeare's lines as prophecy. Gladys asked,
What is my Destiny? The book replied, Take twenty cards
and number them. Gladys stared into a grate,
one brother dead without a grave, another buried
too soon after. Then her daughter, Leonora. Margins
hold her dots, crosses – page fifty-one is dark with grease.
Her hand, (I had her ring) was child-sized and stopped
most often here, at the Oraculum, detailing a firmament
lit with falling stars, storms that follow sea-birds,
omens sung daily by sparrows in the unlucky tree.

'One woe doth tread upon another's heel,
So fast they follow . . .'
Hamlet, Act 4, Scene 7

Something about species

I saw a white deer by the side of the tracks
against a green wall of trees
those seconds alone with her a pardon for leaving

Owl duet above Banyalbufar

The night he arrives, a scops owl greets
a fellow composer. Its call travels to our terrace,

level with the tops of plane and cherry trees,
to three of us aiming binoculars at stars and sea.

As it starts a beat in the canopy he finds
the pitch, note, time. Such old music in the owl

keeping its rhythm, him adding a tune,
the earth their arena, this duet between a veteran

of night calling for a mate and a young man
introducing himself and his love.

Annie

Between explaining solitary bumble bees,
Annie jumps from a garden chair
to point her camera at lavender
bowing under the weight of a pollinator,
always hoping the nearly extinct will appear
in the sun, summoned from the past
where they shelter with an unnamed cast
of insects, the ones that dispose of the dead,
or prismatic beetle gods, all the brocaded,
speckled moths. She's brought vetch,
as if it will transmit wirelessly a message
locked in the earth: *here, here, here is childhood*
with its nettle stings, scrambling yellow flowers
and clover fields, buzzing. *We want you back,* she says.

In a stable

I stood dipping a sponge in a bucket,
soaping a bridle, rinsing grass off a bit,
I tucked stirrups up to the flap of a saddle,
forked straw out of its bale onto the floor
and my first period came. I felt her around
the yard, in my feet flat on concrete,
in someone splashing water from a tap,
in the horses on each side, whinnying.

Celandine in dark wood

Celandine, the first flower
I knew the name of,
grew with white anemones
which died when you picked them.

When Victorian colonists
were afraid of appearing improper –
except when committing genocide,
arranging children at looms –

they spoke a language of flowers.
Joys to come, the lesser celandine
mutters in floriography
on the edge of a dark wood

where a girl was murdered.
Messenger, others call it,
a sign of poor, neglected earth
and see, it's plentiful as stars.

* Lesser celandine vernacular name: spring messenger. Source: *Plantlife*.

The hammock Jane gave me

I roped from the graveyard hedge
to an elder tree, secure but loose

allowing me to sway in a conversation
between branches and sky

the potential of knots and thread
to cradle a body when it's time

Field of cabbage

Folded so neat in a ball, the cabbage
grows almost anywhere, wrapping itself
in layers like a woman who doesn't care.
I kneel to the cabbage and pray.

Invent mutations, I beg,
in your closely packed heart,
new insects, a plague that will jump
to bots, plastic lawns and so on.

The strimming man

The fox appears uphill to stand by a gravestone
still as an angel, his brush to the ground.
He places his silence next to ours.
The three of us, Helen, me, the fox, watch
a strimming man, alone in his head and earbuds
with music to suit the sweeps of his machine.
Green to brown, he moves, transforming grass
to dust. Plastic bouquets blow off graves,
heads roll from him cinematically. The fox pads
to another human memorial, lifts his leg on it,
ignores three crows, and their untranslatable
conversation. *Are they laughing at us?*
Helen asks. The strimming man strims on.

Riverfly census

The towpath's overhung with cow parsley and grasses,
weeping willows bend to the water. The day vibrates with
    flies –
fish break the surface for them, reflections readjust for them.
Mayflies spin across the river, midges spiral into columns
over water meadows that stretch towards another place.
I wave horse flies from my legs. It's the warmest May
and it hasn't happened yet, the time without flies.
The man I love hums. We look for somewhere to lie down.

Hummingbird hawk moth

Lucky, they say, to see one
     and who wouldn't be a hummingbird,

take a chance to hover in feather colours
     above valerian opening?

In the foam of flowers its proboscis
     extends like a drinking straw

into a fishbowl cocktail. *Who wouldn't
     be an imposter, just once,*

I think, when I see one flying
     in sunshine, beautiful, boneless.

It doesn't even have to sing, its only language
     deception, keeping wings

motoring, it might be a body double,
     such mimicry, such tricks.

Wetherspoons

Above Asda, one by one, groups of starlings
are heading towards the flock, quick

above a seafront dense with mist, waves endless,
frothing. The teenage cashier bows his head,

can't let his eyes meet mine, and a family we know
is mourning, a year on. So starlings massing to roost

under Wetherspoons bring young men to mind,
the ones missed, missing, on London, Western Road,

and if I wasn't driving, I'd go down to the water for the song
the birds make in winter, thousands of them safe

under the pub for the night. Down by the water, amplified
by salt, wood and iron, the song drowns everything.

Stag beetle

in the first decade of my life
stag beetles flew
on summer nights

leaving nests in woodpiles
their flight paths
erratic over our stream

drawn to and from pines
behind our house
and napalm roared

through forests in Vietnam
on our tiny black-and-white TV
they shone, fires, beetles

snagged together
in this way by trees
earth, wings – the beetle

summoning thunder
flying for a mate
napalm hurtling towards skin

Cruella de Vil visits Brighton

When I answered the girl's question on the train from Victoria of course, I told her, my fur was real and yes, it was seal with a rare fox collar, my bag alligator, my shoes piglets and how did she think her hideous t-shirt was grown, picked, and where do the dyes go, for her jeans? Into the streams my dear, into mountain streams. She'd throw red on my coat, she said, I dare you, I spat, I'll slit your throat with my nails, deflate you like a lung. The sun shone on my lips and I listened for the song of the whale.

Worm before and after

The worm started to study itself, it had arms, legs, eyes,
brain, it understood microbes, mud, its relationships with
ants, woodlice, it understood the chain of events, it tunnelled
for air, a twisting root, its last words before losing its legs,
arms, eyes, brain, before it tunnelled down, leaving its young
in off-shoots, dead ends, to invite air into the earth to drag
anything dead below it, were *mammals are trouble, you and
your language.*

Species in their millions

Yeah, the ending, it's bound to be bleak.
Her last words. She'd preached of the rise and fall
of the Downs, how a butcherbird instructs its young.
Her fame never found a way out. She summoned chanterelles,
magic mushrooms (revealed where to gather them –
nature's consolation), she called on amoeba,
splashy blobs in the style of Keith Haring.

The five kingdoms fanned into quilts of diaspora
and memoriam. She invented the noon call,
hour of the lost, hour of grief for the golden toad,
seaweeds, grasses, for the palms, reptiles, passenger
pigeons that return only in name and the force
of her lists. Congested by humans, every road to her
was defeated by rumours of a rare passerine.
Or something else – people thinking they're pilgrims,
gaping at relics delivered as memes.

She replaced Flora and Pomona with a little whirlpool
ramshorn snail who made it back from the brink.
It stood beside her with a cloud living spider.
A large gold case bearer brought her yellow. The moth
knew a meadow. She gulped kelp, listened to ripples
speaking to ponds, the forest sounding off.

Choirs of species in their millions begin, conducted
by those who survive, undiscovered, despite us.
In airspace round the tower a soprano pipistrelle
swoops and turns, an oak lutestring leaves a tree
to play the four lines of its wings in the light.

Apple blossom

The year Dylan's mother died
I picked sprays of apple blossom,
wound its pink, off-white shades
in raffia for you to take to him.

Every year it's out I think of us,
the children, how apples bring
the tree so low, until they thud
to the lawn, drumming the end

of summer. The blossom was heavy
when Dylan's mother was dying –
old wood doing its best again –
and he, like you, was so young.

Estuary

our lady of the O

the chant to her
begins with O
the choir repeats O
to summon a redeemer
from her womb

she's a devotion to O
I walk the river path
named for her
reeds practise her name
with the breeze

oars pull in the flow
a swan washes sins away
emptying the O
a dove coos for her
it knows every note of the O

the welcomes and losses she owns
oranges fall from trees for her
their blossom climbs
a stone staircase
enters a window O

Two walks

I've done the chapel alone as penance
for city life and all of my wrongs, up a steep

cobbled path, a pilgrim breathing hard.
Today's track is flatter, lichen grey, fenced

with webs. They sag by the empty cottage.
(Fabrice born '44, dead of Covid).

I'd live there, I joke. *No car, no water?* friends ask.
The valley sinks, woods blur, a village barely awake

has nothing to say. Someone hammers up signs
reading CLOSED and a raven calls

from the hill's dark snout like a dog. It conjures
hunters from last Sunday, shouts, hounds baying

past the house. A painted line by the road
marks a way back – mushrooms we daren't pick,

furrows boar families rooted last night. I met a man
decades ago who lived at a valley's dead end.

He wouldn't leave for war, love, made his nightly
pastis from wild fennel, liquorice, leftover

grape skins. *Too late*, say my friends. The raven
concurs and I answer, *I know, yes I know.*

Avocados

We bought a bag of twenty, local ones,
just ripe, the countryside heaving with them.

Next morning, alone at dawn,
I sliced into the skin, flicked out the stone,

scooping its green flesh, famished.
Among the rocks, trees, undergrowth,

vervet monkeys watched for their turn
at the bag I left on a table, careless.

After all these years, I crave this smooth green
without salt, the mountain behind me,

the stream that once ran out of it –
three avocados, I ate, one by one.

Returning home

The clouds above me are separated into body parts.
I could believe they make the shape of a turtle

or are those flippers wings? It's all I can think about,
the anatomy overhead – vertebrae, flesh turned to feathers,

a disintegrating spine, the jigsaw life is
these days as a turtle becomes a lobster

in patches of evening sky, the estuary below,
reflecting it all without mutation.

It's this I'd like to learn – the estuary's mind
before a city's lights come on to distract me again.

Knowing nothing at all

What I'm told of the house
I was taken to, newborn,

is that it was glorious –
home to friends real and imagined,

there was a high wall to balance on
a circle of standing stones so close.

It took decades to discover
that the town mum lived in

was the same her mother married in.
Mum knew nothing, nothing at all

of this but like her story of our cat
finding its way back to that house –

days and nights trusting its sense of home –
I believe mum navigated by lullaby

until she stood with her own child
in her lost mother's place.

What does it do to me?

This flock of swans on an estuary,
more than I can count

and the heron by the water
near my daughter's flat,

moorhens, ducks, cats skulking,
what does this flatness do?

Not a hill to interrupt my view
only trees weeping into streams,

canals, the pond
at the end of the block weeping too

as I remember the willows
of childhood slung with ropes

to swing over water and fall.
Mud opening its arms.

Open door

The vixen finds a pile of jumpers,
mohair's silky warmth, curls asleep.

I pull a curtain and see her coral coat,
yellow eyes . . . whisper, not quite believing,

gorgeous, you can't stay here.
In her stare, I see the path to my room,

carpet of lions, birds, flowers, vines.
I see her pushing through the reeds

of night to this corner, soft as hay
you'd never want to leave.

Lost

Distracted by a wasteland of yellow flowers
I passed the tower, walked back, passed it again
on the other side – came to another tower, lower, wider.
Gardens stretched beyond a moat. I crossed the same road
three times before I saw a woman with a dog.
I don't know where I am, I said. She smiled.
We might have talked but I spoke her language badly.
She waved her arms, to show the place was close,
pointed, her gestures instructed me to cross again,
turn right, carry straight on. The dog barked to confirm.
I wanted to say *I've been so lost I found a square to empire.*
Fifteen minutes from A to B took two hours. My knack
of reading maps was gone, my south was north, compass broken.
My phone took me in the opposite direction. It held too many
old locations. If I found the river I'd be okay. I believed
I could navigate by smell. I watched a man preach to no one
but himself, and walked again for hours, when it found me.

Floor tile with heart

made to be danced on – a heart with wings
AMOR a trumpet rising between chambers

the paths a heart takes announcing itself in boots
or heels and complicated footwork

how many times is it repeated, the word heart
with the word AMOR both speeding up step by step?

I'm not here

My train cancelled, I count one to ten
like a boy, the seeker, face in his hands.

I'm not here, I'm out of the country
in a café with the sweetest beer

admiring strangers. Twenty-four hours
in hiding, a suitcase packed with champagne

and blackberry jelly flavoured with lemon.
I can't sleep, why waste time – I'm a secret

among friends, lost at the mouth of a river
with water birds, turbines looming over fields.

Blades summon wind like standing stones
calling the sun into line for prayers at dawn.

Acknowledgements

Poems from the collection have appeared in *Spelt*, *Ink Sweat & Tears*, *Artemis Poetry*, *Orbis*, *Under the Radar*, *The Friday Poem*, *New Welsh Review*, *Frogmore Papers*, *ROSA Magazine*, *London Grip*, *The North*, *The Fig Tree*, *The Rialto*, *Pennine Platform*, *boundby*, *Two Ravens* (Grey Hen Press, 2024) and online for the Cholmondeley Awards launch 2024.

Cover image by Jane Sybilla Fordham
https://janesybillafordham.com/
@janesybillafordham

This book has been typeset by
SALT PUBLISHING LIMITED
using Sabon, a font designed by Jan Tschichold
for the D. Stempel AG, Linotype and Monotype
Foundries. It has been manufactured using Holmen
Book Cream 65gsm paper, and printed and bound by
Clays Limited in Bungay, Suffolk, Great Britain.

CROMER
GREAT BRITAIN
MMXXVI